"This generation of Christians inhabit cultures that sometimes reject not only biblical revelation about reality but also the reality of reality itself. The Questions for Restless Minds series poses many of the toughest questions faced by young Christians to some of the world's foremost Christian thinkers and leaders. Along the way, this series seeks to help the Christian next generation to learn how to think biblically when they face questions in years to come that perhaps no one yet sees coming."

—Russell Moore,

public theologian, *Christianity Today*

"The best thing about Sam's book *How Do We Talk with Skeptics?* is not just that it's practical, but it's realistic. Sam anticipates the challenges we will face and shares ten tips to help us overcome them. As you read Sam's tips you will find yourself thinking 'yes—I was wondering how to do that.' As an evangelism trainer, I recommend Sam's tips to others. As a Christian who wants to talk about Jesus with my skeptical friends, I put them into practice."

—Belinda Lakelin,

creator of "Plan A: The Great Commission for Every Christian"
for the Baptist Association of NSW and ACT

T0311432

"Sam Chan is a compass for our complex times, guiding Christians through the culturally-fraught waters of commending Christ to others. The practical wisdom packed into this contribution is indispensable for anyone serious about having better God conversations."

—**Dan Paterson,**
founder of Questioning Christianity; speaker and evangelist;
coauthor of *Questioning Christianity*

"This is seriously awesome! I've read a lot of books on evangelism, and Sam Chan's insight into the culture and the way forward in conversations is profound. What a blessing you are to us all. This is not to be put on the pile of books to be read 'sometime,' but this is one to be read tonight."

—**Julie-anne Laird,**
director of missional engagement, City to City Australia;
canon for church planting, Melbourne Anglican Diocese

"Sam's brilliance is in taking the ordinary situations that we might never have otherwise analysed, and he unpacks them, exposing the underlying dynamic. He takes us behind the scenes and points out the workings backstage with clarity. He offers such great observations about culture today and what is going on in our interactions with unbelievers and in doing so gives us the tools to understand the art of conversation and begin to share Jesus in a natural way. This book is filled with so many ah-ha moments!"

—**Wendy Potts,**
learning consultant in evangelism, Anglicare Sydney

How Do We Talk with Skeptics?

Questions for Restless Minds

Questions for Restless Minds

QUESTIONS FOR RESTLESS MINDS

How Do We Talk with Skeptics?

Sam Chan

D. A. Carson,
Series Editor

LEXHAM PRESS

How Do We Talk with Skeptics?
Questions for Restless Minds, edited by D. A. Carson

Copyright 2021 Christ on Campus Initiative

Lexham Press, 1313 Commercial St., Bellingham, WA 98225
LexhamPress.com

Print ISBN 9781683595212
Digital ISBN 9781683595229
Library of Congress Control Number 2021937695

Lexham Editorial: Todd Hains, Abigail Stocker, Mandi Newell
Cover Design: Brittany Schrock
Typesetting: Abigail Stocker

The Christ on Campus Initiative exists to inspire students on college and university campuses to think wisely, act with conviction, and become more Christlike by providing relevant and excellent evangelical resources on contemporary issues.

Visit christoncampuscci.org.

Contents

Series Preface

D. A. CARSON, SERIES EDITOR

T HE ORIGIN OF this series of books lies with a group of faculty from Trinity Evangelical Divinity School (TEDS), under the leadership of Scott Manetsch. We wanted to address topics faced by today's undergraduates, especially those from Christian homes and churches.

If you are one such student, you already know what we have in mind. You know that most churches, however encouraging they may be, are not equipped to prepare you for what you will face when you enroll at university.

It's not as if you've never known any winsome atheists before going to college; it's not as if you've never thought about Islam, or the credibility of the New Testament documents, or the nature of friendship, or gender identity, or how the claims of Jesus sound too exclusive and rather narrow, or the nature of evil. But up until now you've probably thought about such things within the shielding cocoon of a community of faith.

Now you are at college, and the communities in which you are embedded often find Christian perspectives to be at best oddly quaint and old-fashioned, if not repulsive. To use the current jargon, it's easy to become socialized into a new community, a new world.

How shall you respond? You could, of course, withdraw a little: just buckle down and study computer science or Roman history (or whatever your subject is) and refuse to engage with others. Or you could throw over your Christian heritage as something that belongs to your immature years and buy into the cultural package that surrounds you. Or—and this is what we hope you will do—you could become better informed.

But how shall you go about this? On any disputed topic, you do not have the time, and probably not the interest, to bury yourself in a couple of dozen volumes written by experts for experts. And if you did, that would be on *one* topic—and there are scores of topics that will grab the attention of the inquisitive student. On the other hand, brief pamphlets with predictable answers couched in safe slogans will prove to be neither attractive nor convincing.

So we have adopted a middle course. We have written short books pitched at undergraduates who want arguments that are accessible and stimulating, but invariably courteous. The material is comprehensive enough that it has become an important resource for pastors and other campus leaders who devote their energies to work with students. Each book ends with a brief annotated bibliography and study questions, intended for readers who want to probe a little further.

Lexham Press is making this series available both as attractive books and digitally in new formats (ebook and Logos resource). We hope and pray you will find them helpful and convincing.

INTRODUCTION

F OR THE CHRISTMAS break, I watched *Bumblebee*, which is a fun installment in the *Transformers* franchise. In the final scene, after good has triumphed over evil, the potential boyfriend, Memo (Jorge Lendeborg Jr.), tries to hold the hand of the female hero, Charlie (Hailee Steinfeld). But Charlie smiles and brushes Memo's hand away. She says something like, "No. Not ready." It's a nice way to end the movie because we have the unresolved tension between Charlie and Memo. Will they become girlfriend and boyfriend? At this stage, we won't know.

But at the same time, it shows the dilemma that Memo faces. Right now he's stuck in the dreaded Friendzone. From here, if he overplays his romantic intentions, he will drive her away. But if he underplays his romantic intentions, he will miss out on the opportunity to date her. Maybe she would've loved to be his girlfriend, if only he'd had the courage to ask!

This is similar to the dilemma many of us face as Christians. How can we talk to our nonbelieving, skeptical friends about things that matter? Right now, we're in a similar Friendzone. But we want them to be more than just our friends. We want them also to have the opportunity to know, love, and worship Jesus. But if we overplay this, we risk driving them away. They might never want to have another awkward conversation with us again. But if we underplay this, our friends will never have the chance to hear about Jesus. Maybe they would've gladly believed in Jesus, if only we had told them, but we didn't!

So how can we get the balance right? Let me share with you ten pointers that might help. I'm not saying that they're the best way of doing this. Nor am I saying that they're the only way of doing this, as if you did this any other way you'd be doing it the wrong way. All I'm doing is sharing ten suggestions that are working for me, and maybe they'll also work for you.

BE REALISTIC ABOUT HOW MUCH YOU'LL TALK

RECENTLY I WAS in the hospital for over two weeks as a patient. To pass the time, I watched several of Aaron Sorkin's movies—*A Few Good Men, Molly's Game,* and *The American President.* These movies don't have gunfights, car chases, or a big CGI (Computer-Generated Imagery) fight scene at the end. But what they have is dramatic tension that climaxes in a stirring speech from the lead actor. The speech is the pinnacle of the movie. The speech knocks away all opposition. It is the "drop the mic" moment. But the speech is just as unbelievable as any Hollywood gunfight, car chase, or superhero CGI fight. Because in real life, for a variety of reasons, it just wouldn't happen that way.

Maybe up until now we've pictured the moment we talk to our skeptical friends about Jesus as just like an Aaron Sorkin speech. But I'm here to explain why it probably won't happen that way.[1] That's because there are basically three scenarios for talking to nonbelievers about things that matter, such as the gospel. The first scenario is being invited to give a *public talk*—usually to a "mixed audience" of believers and nonbelievers. For example, in my work with City Bible Forum in Australia, I often give talks at cafés, pubs, and conference rooms to a variety of audiences, ranging from lawyers, traders, accountants, to high-school students. In this scenario, I can monologue for twenty minutes and then answer whatever questions people ask me afterwards. I do almost 90–100 percent of the talking, and the audience knows very little about my personal life, apart from what I tell them. I am also in control of the agenda and direction of the conversation. As a result, the talk is a logical progression of ideas in an ordered and coherent argument. And because my talks are advertised as addressing weighty issues, I can spend most of the time talking about important things—values, worldviews, matters of faith, spirituality, and religion.

In the second scenario, we find ourselves *talking to a stranger*, whom we will never meet again. For example, in my work, I often find myself talking to the Uber driver or the person sitting next to me on the plane. In this scenario, the stranger and I will share the talking—it's a 50–50 percent split. We go back-and-forth. I talk, and they talk. Here, the person still knows very little about my personal life, but they might have some clues as to the person I am. Am I polite to the flight attendant? Did I sit in the front seat or the back seat with the Uber driver? Did I offer to share my snacks? Here, I still have some control of the agenda and direction of the conversation, but so does the other person. As a result, we might flitter between talking about things that matter and things that don't matter all that much—for example, the weather, the sports scores, and what the traffic is like.

In the third scenario, which is the topic of this chapter, we are trying to talk to close *friends and family*, whom we might be stuck with for the rest of our lives. For example, in my work as a medical doctor, most of the doctors and nurses that I work with are nonbelievers. I also have close family members—an uncle, a cousin—who are nonbelievers. In this scenario, things are no longer so straightforward. On the one hand, we have multiple opportunities to have conversations. But on the other hand, if the conversation becomes unpleasant, things will be awkward between us every time that we have to see each other again. Another difficulty is that if we've already had a few conversations about things that matter—the environment, gun control, immigration, the gospel—and they don't agree with us, then it's highly unlikely that they will change their minds just because we bring the matter up again.

In this scenario, the nature of the conversation will be very organic. There is no logical presentation of ideas. Instead, the conversation evolves on its own accord. Furthermore, we may well find that the other person does almost 90–100 percent of the talking. We get to do only 0–10 percent of the talking! The ratio of talking versus listening is completely flipped from what it is to give a public talk. Conversely, they will know almost 100 percent of our personal life. Again, this is completely flipped from what it is when we give a public talk.

Why is this important? Because, as you probably know, the Ancient Greeks taught that there are three components to a message—*logos* (what I say), *pathos* (the way I make you feel), and *ethos* (how I live). When I give a public talk, there is a lot of *logos* and *pathos*, but little *ethos*. But when it comes to talking to close friends and family, *ethos* becomes a huge component in our message.

The Bible has similar insights. For example, in 1 Peter 3:1–2, it says that non-believing husbands can be "won over without words by the behavior of their wives, when they see the purity and reverence of [their] lives." That is to say, in close personal relationships our *ethos*—the way we live—might be much more persuasive than our *logos*—what we say.

So we understand that there is a spectrum of engagements with nonbelievers. Giving a public talk is not the same as talking to a stranger on a plane; and talking to a stranger on a plane is not the same as talking to your roommate about Jesus. As a result, we need to be realistic in our expectations. For example, if we're talking to a close friend, we probably will not be able to give a twenty-minute monologue. And that's OK. We should not be comparing our evangelistic method with Billy Graham's at Wembley Stadium. Nor to an Aaron Sorkin speech!

But even more, it also shows the disproportionately large part that *ethos* plays in personal evangelism. What we say is important. But the more closely someone knows us, the more they will be persuaded by our way of life than merely by what we can say.

	Public Talk	**Talking to a Stranger**	**Friends/ Family**
You Talking	90–100%	50%	0–10%
You Listening	0–10%	50%	90–100%
Your Personal Life Shared	0–10%	20–30%	90–100%
Nature of Conversation	logical, linear, orderly	back-and-forth	organic, unstructured
Type of conversation	one-off monologue	one-off conversation	multiple conversations

2

FIND CREATIVE WAYS TO DO HOSPITALITY

I GREW UP IN Australia. My Asian parents never had roofracks on their cars. That's because Asian parents back then generally didn't surf or go camping. So they had no need for roofracks. So, as a child, I never noticed any roofracks. But now that I'm all grown up, I wanted to buy roofracks for my car. And that's when I noticed that roofracks are everywhere. There are grey ones. There are black ones. There are rounded ones. And there are oblong ones. How did I not notice all of this before?

It's the same with hospitality. For most of my Christian life I hadn't noticed hospitality in the Bible. But now that I go looking for it, hospitality is *everywhere* in the Bible. The word "hospitality" occurs in Acts, Romans, 1 Timothy, Hebrews, 1 Peter, and 3 John. In other words, almost every New Testament writer uses it.

But the idea of hospitality goes beyond the word occurrence. It's there when Zacchaeus welcomes Jesus into his home with joy (Luke 19:5–6). Or when Levi throws a banquet for Jesus and invites his tax-collecting friends (Luke 5:29). It's there when Lydia invites Paul and his entourage to her home (Acts 16:15). Or when the jailer takes Paul and Silas to his home for a meal (Acts 16:34). Interestingly, in many of these examples, it's the nonbeliever who is hospitable to the believer!

But what's the big deal about hospitality? You see, hospitality provides the spaces where conversations occur. In almost every other area of life it's difficult to have a conversation of any weighty matter. Sometimes it's because it's inconvenient—they have a train to catch. Sometimes it's inappropriate—they should be working and not talking to you. Sometimes it goes against social etiquette—it's not the time nor place to talk. But the whole point of a meal together is to talk. The great irony of eating together is that it isn't about the food. It's about connecting. Relating. *And talking*.

There are several things that we can take away from this point about hospitality. First, if a nonbeliever invites us to their home for a meal, we should make it a top priority to go. In Luke 7, we have the story of a woman anointing and washing Jesus' feet with her hair, tears, and perfume. This is a major moment in the story. But it also distracts us from another key moment in the story. And it's this: When Simon the Pharisee invited Jesus to his home for dinner, Jesus *went!* Similarly, in Luke 14:1, Jesus *went* to the house of a prominent Pharisee.

In other words, if our non-believing friends invite us for a dinner, party, fundraiser, or whatever, unless there's a really good reason not to, we should go. Often I hear Christians lamenting that they have no non-believing friends. Or that they don't get to talk to their friends about weighty matters. Maybe a simple solution is to make it foundational to our lifestyle to go to their meals or parties whenever we're invited.

Second, we need to make hospitality foundational to our own lifestyle. I would push this even further to suggest that we need to find creative ways to do hospitality. That's because for many of us, the traditional forms of hospitality are impossible. Maybe we're still living at home with our parents. Or we live in the back of a car! Who knows? But that's where we can find work-arounds. For example, we can order their coffee for them and then pay for it—our treat! Or we can turn up to someone's place with a pizza. Or we can bake a cake and share it. In all of these examples, we still end up creating a space where we eat and drink together. And ultimately end up connecting, relating, and *talking.*

Third, hospitality is a form of generosity. Hospitality is costly. It costs time, effort, and money. But as a result, hospitality gives us social capital. This allows us to talk about matters—matters that our friends might not agree with—but they will give us permission to disagree because we've earned their trust. And if we've been generous to them, then they will most likely be equally generous to us by at least listening to our views, even if they don't agree with what we're saying. Hospitality also makes the host vulnerable— we're opening up our private home to our guests. But in doing so, hospitality invites the guests to be vulnerable in return. This is a safe space where they can talk about private matters that are weighty to their heart.

But if all of the above is true, why do we still hear that there are two things that we must not talk about at a dinner party—namely, politics and religion? In other words, there seems to be a mantra that we should *not* talk about weighty matters over a meal. Instead, so we hear, we should only talk about safe subjects such as the weather and what TV shows we've watched lately. I think that this is because people often don't know how to disagree well. So, how can we talk about weighty matters and disagree well at the same time? The next few points might help.

3

LEARN THE
ART OF
CONVERSATION

D O YOU EVER find yourself talking about the weather and wondering why? Why are we so obsessed with asking each other about our weekend? Or why does the other person always ask about what my plans are for the vacation? Or why do they tell me to say "hi" to my wife and kids, when they could just pick up the phone and do it themselves?

To understand this, we need to grasp that there are layers to a conversation, similar to the layers of an onion:

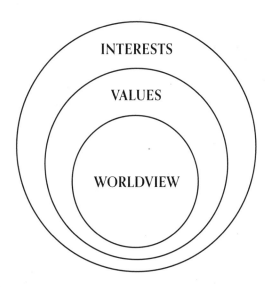

Usually conversations begin in the outer layer of *interests*. What did you do on the weekend? What are you watching on Netflix? What are your plans for the vacation? What subjects are you taking? What do you hope to do for work? Who's your NFL team? What movies do you enjoy watching? Where's home for you?

That's because, in this layer, the statements will be *descriptive*. They merely describe factual statements that are, by and large, seemingly easy to verify. For example, if I ask you what are your plans for the holidays, and you tell me that you plan to go fishing in Michigan, I'm not going to say, "I disagree!" If I ask you what you're watching on TV, and you tell me that it's *Game of Thrones*, I'm not going to say, "No, I don't believe you—you're lying!" And if I ask you what movies you enjoy watching, and you tell me that you enjoy James Bond movies, I'm not going to say, "No you don't!" Or if I ask you what is your NFL team, and you tell me it's the Chicago Bears, I'm not going to say, "I think you're wrong about that." As a result, this is a safe layer for conversations. The talk will be civil. There will be little chance of disagreement.

But in the middle layer, we enter the world of *value* statements. We make statements about preferences, ethics, value, and beauty. For example, in this layer, our friend might say, "Fishing is a cruel thing to do to the fish." Or they might say, "There's too much misogyny in *Game of Thrones*." Or they might say, "James Bond movies are better than rom-coms." Or they might say, "The football in the NCAA is superior to that in the NFL."

In this layer, the statements are *prescriptive*. They have a sense of oughtness. They describe evaluative claims that are, by and large, difficult to verify immediately. As a result, there will be a high chance of disagreement. You might want to take the opposite side of the argument—fishing is not cruel, *Game of Thrones* is about female empowerment, rom-coms are better than James Bond, and the NFL is better than the NCAA!

This is why we find it difficult to have conversations about weighty matters. It is not because we lack courage, and not because we lack opportunities, but, because, in general, these conversations will end badly. There will be conflicting views. And there are friendships at stake!

But if that's challenging enough, wait until we hit the central layer of conversations, where we start talking about *worldviews*. Here we make statements about what we believe to be reality itself. Is there a God? Is there life after death? Are humans good or evil? Are we individuals or a collective? Is there free will? What is the meaning of life? Is this all that there is?

For example, in this layer, our friend might say, "Fishing is cruel because there is no difference between a fish and a human being." Or they might say, "*Game of Thrones* shows us that the arc of history ultimately bends toward freedom." Or they might say, "James Bond movies only make sense if you believe in good versus evil, but I think there is no such thing." Or they might say, "The NCAA is superior because the players play as a team, but the NFL is too much about individualism."

Our worldviews are the engine room that generate and drive our values. They are the interpretive lenses for how we understand the world of facts. As a result, if we have different worldviews, we don't just disagree, we actually *disconnect*. We are sitting on two different mountaintops with two different ways of understanding reality, two different ways of interpreting the evidence. For example, if our friend doesn't believe in life after death, then it might make perfect sense to maximize the amount of happiness in this lifetime. Or if they believe that humans are just another species of life on this earth, it makes sense not to privilege our species over that of another.

So what has all of this to do with the art of conversation? First, we can learn to recognize which layer we're in. Don't be afraid of so-called small talk. Small talk is merely talk that's in the outside layer of *interests*. It sounds superficial, but it functions as a safe area for conversation that won't lead to disagreements or conflict.

Second, if we are good at listening, and earn enough trust while talking about *interests*, bit by bit, those with whom we are talking will move the conversation into the layer of *values*. They might even move the conversation into the layer of *worldviews*. A friend of mine who was training as a hospital chaplain told me that a person will actually drop hints that they're ready to move the conversation onto the next layer. Our job is to listen intently, pick up on the cues, and simply ask questions like, "Tell me about that," or "How did that make you feel?" That will give them permission to take us into the next layer.

Third, conversely, we ourselves may take the initiative to move the conversation into the next layer. We do this simply by asking questions. For example, if we ask them what they did on the weekend, and they say they played basketball, we are in the *interests* layer of the conversation. But if we then ask, "Why do you play basketball on the weekends?" To answer this they will have to move into the *values* layer. For example, they might say, "It keeps me healthy." And then if we ask, "Why do we value health so much?" To answer this they will have to move into the *worldviews* layer. For example, they might say, "We only live once, so I want to live for as long as possible."

Or, fourth, we can simply move straight to worldviews. In the same way that questions such as "What did you do on the weekend?" immediately lead to the *interests* layer of conversations, there are other questions that will immediately lead to the *worldviews* layer of conversations. For example, try these questions: "Do you have a faith?", "What religion did your parents raise you with?",[2] or "Do you pray?"[3] I have found that these questions are safe questions to ask because, on the surface, they are still *descriptive*. We're merely asking a factual question. But, on the other hand, they invite the person to share their worldview—in particularly their views on the spiritual and the sacred—with us. I have found that, when I do this, sometimes the person will show that they simply don't want to talk about this. And that's OK. We offered them a chance to talk about things that matter to them and they didn't want to open up to us yet. But on many other occasions, I've found that people welcome an opportunity to talk about things that are deepest and most valuable to them.

4

LEARN THE ART
OF LISTENING

I REMEMBER HOW, MANY years ago, I had to make a major decision in my life. So I visited a lot of friends and asked for their advice. To my dismay, when I visited each one of them, they just talked and talked to me. They gave me their advice. Isn't that what I asked them for? Isn't it what I wanted? Well, it's what I thought I wanted, until I sat on the receiving end of a monologue. What I realize now, but I didn't know back then, was that I wanted to be heard. I actually wanted someone to talk to, rather than to be talked at. What they said to me might have been very wise advice, but I found it really unhelpful, because what I wanted most of all was for them to listen to me.

In contrast, only a few years ago I saw a professional counselor. She spent easily more than 90 percent of each session letting me talk and talk. Occasionally, she would chip in with a few of her insights. But for most of the time, she would ask a question here and there, and then let me freely talk. I found this whole process to be supremely helpful because, even though I didn't realize it, I really wanted to talk. And, in talking, it opened me up to her suggestions.

So the lesson we can learn from this is that the art of conversation is actually also the art of getting the other person to do most of the talking. A friend of mine, James, who has been trained in counseling, tells me that his technique is simply *not* to talk. If there's a long, uncomfortable pause in the conversation, James says he takes a sip from his cup of drink as a nonverbal signal to the other person that he is not going to talk and that the other person needs to start talking again.

But what are we doing while the other person is talking? We are trying to do three things—*hear, understand*, and *feel*. I often jokingly say that this is everything that us guys were taught in premarital counseling on how to manage conflict with our wives. For example, if my wife says to me, "You haven't been cleaning the dishes." The first thing I need to do is to demonstrate that I have *heard* what she is saying. So I need to say something like, "From what I *hear* you saying I'm not cleaning the dishes. Have I heard you correctly?"

The second thing I need to do is to demonstrate that I have *understood* what she is saying. Here I need to summarize her words in my own words. This demonstrates that I'm not merely parroting her words back to her, but that I've engaged in some sort of analysis of what she has been saying. So I need to say something like, "I *understand* how that means I haven't been doing my share of the housework; would that be how you also see it?"

The third thing I need to do is to demonstrate that I empathize with her emotions. Here I need to describe what she is *feeling*. So I need to say something like, "That must make you *feel* very angry." The funny thing is my wife once caught me giving this advice to my guy friends, and she said to me, "Oh, if I ever catch you doing that to me I'll be so angry!" So I jokingly replied, "From what I hear you saying... " and the joke works because the fourth thing I also need to do is restore trust. I need to say something, "What can I do to earn your trust again?" Her eye roll will tell me that maybe I can at least begin with cleaning the dishes!

But, seriously, while our non-believing friend is talking, we can use this method to engage in what's called "active listening." For example, if we allow our friend to talk at length about their views on, say, same-sex marriage, we might find ourselves saying this when they're finished: "From what I *hear* you saying, you're very much for same-sex marriage. I *understand* how for you this is a matter of justice and equality. So you must *feel* angry when you hear that Christians might not share your point of view. It's going to take a lot before you *trust* Christians. Have I heard you correctly?"

If we do this, we have earned enough capital to be able to speak. Our friend might ask us for our thoughts. Or we might politely ask, "Would you like me to respond?" And if our friend feels that they have been heard, then they will now be open to hearing from us.

5

LEARN THE ART OF PRESENTING OUR POINT OF VIEW

A WHILE AGO, AS a challenge, I thought that it'd be a good idea to learn how to play chess. That's when I discovered that there are three phases to a chess game—the *fore* game, the *mid* game, and the *end* game. In the fore game, you set up your pieces so that they are in strong positions. In the mid game, you try to advance your pieces. In the end game, you try to corner your opponent. It sounded so simple. But I found I never knew what to do after the first phase—the fore game. That's because at this moment I was as safe as I could possibly be with all my pieces set up in front of me. I didn't dare move another piece, to begin the mid game, because to do so automatically opened me up, making me vulnerable.

But here's the thing. In order to move ahead, we have to make ourselves open to attack. So how can we do this in the art of conversation? After we've done all this listening, what do we do when it's our turn to speak? How can we best present what we believe to be true? There are several good options to choose from. First, I can say, "As a follower and believer in the Jesus of the Bible, I have the same view as Jesus." The advantage of this approach is that, in the current Western cultural narrative, authority figures—such as the church—are viewed as oppressive because they impose their metanarratives upon us. But for some reason, our Western culture does not lump Jesus in the same category as the institutionalized church. Instead, Jesus himself is viewed as some sort of subversive, countercultural hero. Another advantage is that it places the basis of our belief upon Jesus. We don't believe what we believe because this is what we prefer to be true. We believe what we believe because this is what Jesus himself tells us is true.

So if my friend says something like, "So what are your views on same-sex marriage?" I can reply by saying that I have the same view as that of Jesus. For example, Jesus believed in true inclusion by eating and drinking with those who disagreed with him. After all, if we only eat with those who agree with us then we're practicing exclusion by excluding those who disagree with us. Jesus also believed in unconditional love by telling his followers to love and bless those who disagreed with them. But Jesus tells his followers to especially love those who disagree with them. That is the mark of a true follower of Jesus. So if we believe in true inclusion and unconditional love, then we also have to be able to disagree with each other. But what is the basis of our disagreement? When it comes to issues of sex and morality, we all believe that some forms of sex are good, but there are other forms of sex that are wrong. In other words, we all have sexual norms, whether we realize it or not. But how do we decide where that line is drawn? What is the basis for our norms? As followers of Jesus, we believe that Jesus is the basis for our norms. Jesus is the one who loved us, made us, and he gets to tell us what to do. This is where I like to point out that, on an issue such as same-sex marriage, if we're disagreeing, it's not over issues of love, inclusion, or human rights. If we're disagreeing, it's over what Jesus tells us is normative.

Second, alternatively, I can say, "Let me tell you something from the Bible." The advantage of this approach is that most of our non-believing friends have no idea what's in the Bible. They might have some poor caricatures of what they think the Bible says, but they've never actually read or heard the Bible for themselves. But if we give them a chance to hear from the Bible, they will discover for themselves how fresh, disarming, and countercultural the Bible's message is. Moreover, I tend to tell them a story from the Bible, because this allows them to imagine the Bible's worldview, rather than merely give them an argument to argue against.

So if my friend says something like, "What's it like to be a Christian?" I can tell them a story about Jesus from the Bible. Depending on the context, I might tell them the story of Jesus healing the paralyzed man who was lowered through the roof on a mat by his friends (Luke 5:17–26). Afterwards I might ask them, "Why would Jesus do that?" and see what my friend says. Or, in another context, I might tell them the story of Jesus turning water into wine (John 2:1–12). I love this story, because it's so disarming! What on earth is Jesus doing—giving so much good wine to people who had already drunk enough? It's not what we would do. So I ask them, "Why would Jesus do that?" After my friend has had a go trying to answer, they will probably then want me to tell them what I think is the answer. I usually say something like, "Partly Jesus did this to give us an image of what life is like with Jesus both now in this life and in the life to come. So if you think that by following Jesus in this life, you will miss out, you're wrong. It's actually the opposite. By *not* following Jesus in this life you will miss out." And then I see where the conversation might go from there.

Or sometimes I like to tell the story that Jesus tells about the Pharisee and the tax collector (Luke 18:9–14). Afterwards, I explain that the Pharisee's prayer today would sound like this: "Dear God, I thank you that I'm better than most people. I give my money to charity. I don't cheat on my wife. I go to all of my children's plays, concerts, and awards nights. And I go to church twice on Sundays—both the traditional and contemporary services." So I ask my friends, "Why does he not get saved, according to Jesus?" After they have a go trying to answer, they will probably want to hear my answer. I can then say something like, "We often think of sin as breaking laws. But for most of the part, Jesus explains sin as being puffed up. It's that feeling we all get when we recycle. Or when we brag about our family in a Christmas newsletter. Or when we turn off our lights on Earth Day." Then I can ask them, "So what do you think the tax collector did to get saved?" After they have a go at answering, I can say something like, "According to Jesus, it's because the tax collector humbled himself and trusted in God." Then I can say that being a Christian is all about being humble. On the one hand, it's humbling. But, on the other hand, it's the most empowering thing ever, because it's about what God has done for us, which is more than what we can ever do for ourselves.

Third, as another option, I can share a personal story. The advantage of this is that stories are naturally engaging. They win over the emotion. They appeal to experience. Nobody can argue against a story. So if my non-believing friend asks me, "What about those who haven't heard about Jesus?" I usually tell them the story about my friend Michael. I tell them how I went through Bible college with Michael. Michael grew up in Iran, which was closed to Christianity. He had no access to the Bible, churches, or the Christian message. But one night, Jesus came to Michael in a dream, and ever since that day, Michael has believed in Jesus. I can also tell them about Sharon (name changed) who was from China. I met her on a tour group in Israel and asked her how she became a Christian. She told me that, while she was living in China, Jesus appeared to her in a dream. But ever since she became a Christian, went to church, and had access to the Bible, Jesus has no longer come to her in a dream. The dreams have stopped. From these stories I tell people, "I believe that God finds creative ways of making himself known, especially to those without access to the Bible. But, according to Jesus, the Bible is the clearest message about God that there is (Luke 16:31). So, for those of us with access to the Bible, God doesn't have to find these creative ways. After all, we've got the Bible!"

Fourth, we can appeal to the Christian point of view. How can I do this? I usually begin by beginning from their point of view. I can say something like, "I get it. I totally get it. If all we are is atoms and molecules. If we're just another species of life on this planet. If there is no God. And if we only live once. Then everything you say makes perfect sense, and I would believe exactly what you also believe." But then I tell them that I come from a different starting point. Here is when I give them the Christian worldview, but using a very simple three-point framework. I once heard Timothy Keller use this, and I've expounded upon it in my book *Evangelism in a Skeptical World*. Basically the three points are (1) manger, (2) cross, and (3) king. That is to say, (1) Jesus came to us as a human; (2) he died for us on the cross; and (3) one day he will return and set up his kingdom on earth.

So, I could say something like this: "I believe in a God who loves me, made me, and saves me. He sent his Son Jesus into our world as a human 2,000 years ago. Jesus died for us on a cross, to take away our guilt and shame. But more than this, one day he's going to come back and set up a physical kingdom here on earth. So in the meantime, I am part of his mission to bring his love, mercy, and justice on this planet. So, can you see how if these things are true, then it completely changes how we might view things?"

The advantage of this approach is that the lights might come on for my friend. Up until now, they thought I was disagreeing with them because I was a religious jerk. But, hopefully, now they can see that the level of disagreement is much more *meta* than that. We are disagreeing because we have completely different starting points. We have completely different ways of viewing reality. And there's no reason why their version of reality should be privileged over my version.

Fifth, we can ask, "What would it take for you to trust Jesus?" Here is where we find what our friend's real objection is. It might be the historical reliability of the Bible. It might be the scientific problem of miracles. But often it will be something more profoundly personal, emotional, and existential. Maybe they've been hurt by the church. Or maybe their mother died of cancer and they're still angry at God. Or maybe they can't follow Jesus if it means betraying the social group to which they find their identity.

6

GENTLY
DISMANTLE
THEIR
WORLDVIEW

B UT, AGAIN, WHY should we have to do all the talking? I once heard a bi-vocational Christian pastor say that when he was in his secular work, he was constantly being bombarded with questions. As a result, he was always answering these questions as best he could in order to explain the Christian faith. But it also meant that he was always on the defensive. So one day, he switched it around. He started asking questions to his work friends. Suddenly they were on the defensive, having to defend and explain their positions. That's when the Christian pastor realized that everyone is only two "why" questions away from not being able to give a rational answer. If we do this—i.e., start asking questions—our non-believing friends will realize that much of their worldview is based, not on rational arguments or evidence, but on brute-force statements that they believe at face value as *a priori* true.

In the Bible, Jesus often does the same thing. He doesn't answer. Instead he asks a question in return. When he's asked to give his views on taxes, he throws a question back, "Show me a denarius. Whose image and inscription are on it?" (Luke 20:24). When he is asked from where he gets his authority, he replies, "I will ask you a question. Tell me: John's baptism—was it from heaven, or of human origin?" (20:3–4).

What questions can we ask? First, we can ask them where they get their views on human rights and dignity from? If I am a Christian, I can derive human rights and dignity from us being created in the image of God. Or I can point to Christ's incarnation—the Son of God became one of us! Or I can appeal to Jesus saying, "Whatever you did for one of the least of these brothers and sisters of mine, you did for me" (Matt 25:40).

But if I don't hold the Christian worldview, where can I derive human rights and dignity from? All I can do is clutch to human laws and conventions. But these are arbitrary social constructs. And they are Western social constructs. So if I speak of human rights and dignity, I'm actually guilty of imposing my Western values upon other cultures that don't hold to similar views. Without a God who transcends human conventions, the belief in universal human rights and dignity will be reduced to another form of Western imperialism.

Similarly, second, we can ask them where they get their views on human equality. Right now, in Western culture, we champion the weak, the poor, and the marginalized. But why ought this be so? Where did this notion come from? Did it just drop out of the sky to us? But if I hold to the Christian worldview, I can appeal to how the God of the Bible is the champion of the underdog—Abel over Cain, Sarah over Hagar, Jacob over Esau, Leah over Rebecca, Israel over the nations. I can point out how Jesus hung out with the marginalized. Or how Jesus, the Son of God, lowered himself and became a slave who died an outcast's death on a cross (Phil 2:5–8)!

But if I don't have this Christian worldview, how can I defend my views on human equality? I can't appeal to Mother Nature or to the animal kingdom. Animal behavior and society are brutally hierarchical. I can't appeal to this being hardwired into us as part of our evolutionary instincts. Even if this were true in the past, why *ought* it continue to be true for me, the individual, in the present? Moreover, our ideas of human equality are very Western. If I impose these views, aren't I guilty again of another form of Western cultural superiority?

Again, third, we can ask them why we can believe in human freedom. Freedom is almost the chief idol of the West. It's enshrined in our national anthems (France, the United States, Australia, Canada, etc.). It's in the US Declaration of Independence. It's in the French Revolution's motto *Liberté, Egalité, Fraternité.* But apart from mottos and national anthems, where do we get the idea that humans ought to be free? At least, if I have a Christian worldview, I can appeal to God who created freely, and gave human beings choices, responsibilities, and free will. I can point out that the word "free" appears almost 200 times in the Bible. I can appeal to Jesus Christ, who comes to set us free (Luke 4:18; John 8:32). Indeed, salvation in the Bible is construed as freedom (Rom 6:7).

But what if I don't believe in God? What is freedom? If we are nothing but atoms and molecules, then we can only be living in a mechanical universe of cause and effect. This is a universe of *determinism*, where freedom is only an illusion. And yet, we hold people accountable for their choices. Witness the recent #MeToo movement and calling out culture. The very premise of these movements is that humans do indeed have freedom and can make morally accountable choices. But where does this freedom come from if there is no God?

Moreover, we talk about freedom as freedom *from* constraints. That is to say, we ought to be free from traditional constraints of religion, social norms, and pressures to conform. But without God, once these constraints are removed, we have no idea what we're free *for*. What exactly are we supposed to do with our freedom? We are rudderless. We have no direction. This is because we actually don't know why we're here on this planet. If there is no God, and we're here by random, blind, chance, then any talk of purpose is meaningless. And, worse, if we don't have to be here, it's only a small leap to start talking about how we shouldn't be here. We're only in the way of other, more important life forms.

So what are we free *for*? To answer this requires knowing our purpose. But any talk of purpose requires knowing our design. A watch's purpose is to tell time, because that is what it's designed for. A pen's purpose is to write, because that is what it's designed for. A lamp's purpose is to give light, because that is what it's designed for. Without design, any talk of purpose is meaningless. And so, if we are to have any sense of purpose, we need to know what is our design. But to do this requires knowing our Designer. This is why Jesus claims to give us freedom (John 8:32). We will not only be set free *from* constraints, but we will also know what we're set free *for.* This is because if we know Jesus, we will know our Designer. And our chief purpose is to be fulfilled in Jesus.

Our friend might reply that they can create their own purpose. Purpose can come from within, rather than from an external source. But we can then gently point out that the problem with this is that any talk of purpose ultimately requires an external reference point. Otherwise we will play a game of infinite regress. For example, if my friend says that the purpose of life is to raise children, I can ask *why?* They might say that it's so the children can be happy. But I can ask *why.* In the end, whatever they pursue—success, happiness, status—is purposeless unless it connects with a bigger story than just their own.

Trying to create our own purpose is like a nation that just prints money. You can't generate wealth just by printing money. The money by itself has no value unless it's linked to an external reference point. In the same way, we can't create our own purpose. We can try, but ultimately it will be valueless unless we can link it to an external reference point—i.e., God's purpose for us.

Fourth, we can gently challenge the current cultural narrative. Right now, in the West, secularism is the unchallenged norm. The narrative goes something like this. We once believed in God, fairies, and unicorns. But as we became more and more enlightened we became rational and stopped believing in the supernatural. And so, if we can subtract away our past superstitious beliefs, and realize that we're only atoms and molecules, then we can be free to be who we really are. The only thing holding us back are those who still haven't got with the program yet—i.e., religious people who still believe in God, who continue to oppress us with their outdated beliefs, traditions, and morals. But if we can courageously be true to ourselves, we will discover the authentic selves within, and we can discover and pursue our full potential. Chase your dreams and don't let anyone else tell you who to be. More than this, this is the arc of history—i.e., humankind will become more and more free to pursue happiness on its own terms. We can either join the progressives along this storyline or be left behind on the "wrong side of history."

We should applaud the many positives in this narrative. For example, for many of us, we are who we are because of this storyline. We didn't have to follow our father's footsteps and do the same job he did; instead, we could choose to do what we loved. We didn't have to stay in the town of our birth; instead, we were free to move to another town for study or work. We didn't have to marry someone from our own tribe or race; instead, we could choose our own romantic partners.

But at the same time, there are a few things that we can gently critique in this narrative. For a start, this narrative is an over-the-top Western narrative of rugged individualism, egalitarianism, and privilege. It assumes we can make choices that for many people, both inside and outside the US, are just impossible. What if the hospital cleaner wants to be an astronaut? Should she leave her job—which is paying the bills and putting her kids through college—just to chase her dreams? Is she any less authentic—or less true to herself—for being a cleaner?

Worse, this narrative is another example of Western cultural superiority and triumphalism. Its very premise is that this Western cultural story is superior to any other culture's storyline. To talk about an arc of history, or progress, or enlightenment, let alone a wrong side of history, is sheer cultural arrogance. What are we basing this superiority on? That we know best? That we are the most recent blip in the timeline of the universe? That we are more "civilized"? We heard all of these same arguments two hundred years ago during Western colonialism, and yet here we are repeating them all over again.

Moreover, this narrative works only if we stay in our tiny Western bubble. Right now, secularism is declining all over the world. Christianity is the fastest growing religion. Millions and millions of people, especially in the majority world—Africa, Asia, and Latin America—are choosing to love, worship, and follow Jesus. So what are they seeing in Jesus that we, in the West, are missing? So I would suggest to my non-believing friends in the West that maybe it's time that we rediscovered the Jesus of the Bible. Forget about the Jesus that we think we know or grew up with. Let's go to the Bible and discover the Jesus that the rest of the world is coming to know. And if we have any problems with the Bible, maybe they are our Western cultural objections, which the rest of the world just doesn't have. And if we think Christianity is a tool of oppression, that is also probably only our Western presuppositions, because the rest of the world is discovering a freedom that comes from knowing the Jesus of the Bible.

I like to make a self-deprecating joke about Asian tourists in Europe, because they stay in their tourist buses with other Chinese tourists, only talking Chinese to each other, and only venturing out of the bus to eat at Chinese restaurants—and then they complain that it's not as good as the food back home! But then someone pointed out to me that the English tourists do the same thing. They also stay in their tourist buses with other English tourists, only talking English to each other, and only venturing out of the bus to eat at Irish pubs—and then they complain that the Guinness is not as good as the one back home! But then someone else pointed out to me that American tourists also do the same thing. They stay in their tourist buses with other Americans, only talking to other Americans, venturing out of the bus only to eat at McDonald's—and then they complain that the Big Mac is not as good as the one back home!

What is my point? As long as the tourists stay in their bubbles, they will never see their own cultural presuppositions and biases. And they will never truly experience the host country's culture, language, peoples, and food. But then I like to point out to my non-believing friends that we often make the same mistake with Jesus and the Bible. We stay in our Western bubbles, and are not aware of our presuppositions and biases. And so we never truly experience the Jesus of the Bible on his own terms. Maybe we should leave our bubble and try to see what the rest of the world is seeing in Jesus.

7

LEARN
THE ART OF
POSITIVE
APOLOGETICS

I N THE PAST, there was a lot of talk about defeater beliefs—
beliefs that our non-believing friends have that supposedly
defeat our Christian beliefs. For example, the usual culprits
in our post-Christian Western culture are: How can you
trust the Bible? What about other religions? Why can't
God just forgive? What are your views on sex and morality? How can God allow suffering? Aren't Christians just
hypocrites? Hasn't science disproved the Bible?

These defeater beliefs are very culture-dependent. For
example, if you were in Taiwan, the defeater belief might
be: "But what about my parents? I can't change religions
because this will cause them too much public shame and
grief." Or if you were in a more traditional culture, the
defeater belief might be: "I've gone to church all my life;
that's enough to get me into heaven."

I believe that all Christians should at least be aware of
what defeater beliefs exist for our non-believing friends
in their particular culture. And I'm sure most of us have
already worked out some helpful ways of responding to
these defeater beliefs. In addition, Timothy Keller's *Reason
For God* is an excellent resource for responding to the
above defeater beliefs. Further, it's helpful if we also let
our non-believing friend know how culturally-specific their
objections are. If our friend lived in another time or place,

they wouldn't have such objections. They would have different ones, of course, but their current objections are very much determined by their cultural locatedness.

But in the last five to ten years, I believe that our culture has become even more post-Christian, to the extent that the above defeater beliefs might not even be an issue. Our friends aren't nonbelievers because the above defeater beliefs are stopping them from believing. Our friends are nonbelievers because they don't even know why they need to believe in the Christian God of the Bible.

Because of this, I think we need to move beyond responding to defeater beliefs—i.e., engaging in negative apologetics—to giving reasons that promote belief—i.e., engaging in positive apologetics. To do this, I like to show my non-believing friend reasons why they need or want Christianity to be true.

For example, I might say, "If you want to believe that a husband ought to love his wife, and not treat her as mere property, you need the God of the Bible to be true. Because I dare you to prove to me, based on any other premise, that a husband ought to love his wife." Whatever reasons they might try to give—for example, it's a good thing to do, it's the right thing to do, a woman has dignity—I can gently respond, "That's simply question-begging. You're merely repeating the starting premise in different words. But so far, you still haven't given me a reason or argument why a husband ought to love his wife. You're merely giving me assertions but not reasons."

As another example, I can do the same thing with human rights. I might say, "If you want to believe in universal human rights—that things like slavery and the sex trade are wrong—then you need the God of the Bible to be true. Because I dare you to prove to me, based on any other premise, that a human being has an inherent dignity, value, or worth, apart from what they achieve or acquire in this life." They might try to give reasons—such as the United Nations' Universal Declaration of Human Rights—but these are all arbitrary human social conventions. And not all cultures and nations hold these to be true. So I can gently respond that unless there's a God who creates us as inherently worthy—in his image—and confers dignity to us by becoming one of us and dying for us, then it's very hard to believe in such a thing as human rights. I can also point out how unique this is to the Judeo-Christian worldview. I'm not aware of any other religious worldview where God or the gods value the life of each and every human. In fact, it's quite the contrary. In most other religions, the gods don't care about the humans. At best, the gods might be coerced into being merciful to the humans every now and then; but at worst, the gods see the human race as an inconvenience.

As another example, I like to say that we like to believe that God is a loving God. In fact, this is the starting premise to most of our objections against the Christian worldview. For example, "How can a loving God allow suffering?" Or, "How can a loving God send people to hell?" Or, "How can a loving God not accept me for who I am?" But I like to ask gently, "Where do we get the idea that God needs to be loving?" We actually only get it from the Judeo-Christian worldview. In no other religion, is God obligated to be loving. In fact, again, it's quite the contrary. In other religions, the gods are simply uncaring, or so sovereign and transcendent that love is bypassed. Or worse, they can be mischievous, malicious, or capricious—trying to work against our best intentions rather than with them. So, if we want to hold to the premise that God is obligated to be loving, then we actually also need the God of the Bible to be true.

Tim Keller's recent book *Making Sense of God* uses a similar approach to what we're doing here. Whereas his book *The Reason for God* was focused on addressing defeater beliefs, *Making Sense of God* is focused on promoting reasons why we need God to be true. In this book, Keller shows how much of what we believe to be true—for example, meaning, satisfaction, freedom, self, identity, hope, morality, and justice—are nonsensical unless the God of the Bible is also true. They cannot exist without a transcendent God who made us, loves us, and saves us. I believe we can similarly use this approach in the art of positive apologetics.

8

USE WISDOM AS AN ENTRY POINT

RECENTLY I HOSTED a BBQ at my place for a bunch of friends. As we sat in the backyard, enjoying the beef brisket and pulled pork, the guests started to admire my green, lush lawn. Soon my friends expressed their wish that their lawns could also look like mine and they started to ask for my advice on how to manage lawns. What time of the year should they fertilize their lawns? How did I get rid of my weeds? After a while, I had a ready audience that was hanging on all my words!

But in my group of friends was also a guy called Adam. Adam had once been a professional landscaper. He also started to talk about lawns. He explained to us the different types of grass, what time of the day was best for watering the lawns, and what height the lawns should be mowed in winter and summer. He was obviously very knowledge-able and experienced in lawn care. Soon he had all of us, including me, under his spell. We enjoyed listening to him and egged him on with more and more questions about lawn care.

What just happened at the BBQ? Which layer of conver-sation were we in? Was it interests, values, or worldviews? The conversation began in the layer of interests—describ-ing my lawn—but soon it moved to a different category. We were prescribing what to do with a lawn. But to say we were in the layer of values doesn't seem to be the right fit. It was something slightly different. We were discussing how to manage a lawn. To water or not to water? To fertilize or not to fertilize? To weed or not to weed? I want to argue that we were in a unique layer of conversation called wisdom.

Wisdom has been an underexplored area of Christian conversation. Often when we think of talking about "things that matter" we think of values, truth, and salvation. As a result, Christians end up being stereotyped, fairly or unfairly, as people who are outspoken on issues of sex and morality, heaven and hell. Part of this is because the Bible spends a lot of time on these issues.

But the Bible also has large sections on wisdom. In the Old Testament we find this in what is traditionally called wisdom literature—Job, Psalms, Proverbs, Ecclesiastes, and Song of Solomon. In the New Testament, we can find similar sections, for example, in Jesus' teachings (e.g., the Sermon on the Mount), Paul's advice in the second parts of his letters, and the book of James.

Knowing God's wisdom is more than knowing what's true or false, or right and wrong. It's knowing what is most apt in a particular circumstance. For example, sometimes the wise thing to do is to answer a fool according to their folly (Prov 26:5). But at other times the wise thing to do is *not* to answer a fool (26:4). So which is it? Here the question is not so much what is true or right but what is wise!

So how can we know this wisdom? In one sense, wisdom is part of God's general revelation both to those who are saved and to those who are not yet saved, to those within and those outside of God's family. This is because God has programmed his wisdom into his creation (Prov 8) so that it should be accessible to all. As a result, though not in each and every case, those who observe God's wisdom in his creation will be able to live according to God's creational design and prosper appropriately. For example, a good friend will be trustworthy (27:6). This goes with God's creational design. We can easily imagine how, as a general rule, this person's friendship will prosper—the friends will enjoy each other's loyalty, support, and commitment in times of plenty and adversity (17:17). In contrast, a foolish, untrustworthy, gossiping friend will go against God's creational design and cause much hurt (16:28). In this case we can imagine how, by and large, this person's friendship will not prosper, and most likely it will end in ruin. As another example, a diligent worker will be able to support themselves and pay the bills (Prov 6). This is part of God's creational design. But workers who are lazy or untrustworthy go against the wisdom programmed by God into his creation. As a result, such a worker will find themselves, more often than not, in financial difficulty. You don't have to be saved by God to know that this is wise advice.

But in another sense, we can argue that the wisdom sections of the Bible make sense only if we assume the Christian worldview and a prior relationship with God inside his kingdom. This is because wisdom is part of God's special revelation addressed to those already within God's family.

After all, wisdom literature itself argues that the "fear of the Lord" is the beginning of wisdom (e.g., Prov 1:7). To know Jesus is to know God's wisdom (1 Cor 1:24). Here, a Christian friend will be trustworthy because they are redeemed by Christ to be so (John 15:13–15). Without Christ, we will be on the wrong side of the curses in Genesis 3, where the human relationships are doomed to conflict (v. 16). But with Christ we begin the journey to God's new creation vision. Similarly, a Christian worker will work diligently because they are now ultimately working for Christ (Col 3:22–25). Without Christ, we stay on the wrong side of the curses in Genesis 3, where our work will be frustrated (vv. 17–19). But with Christ, our work has purpose and will ultimately be rewarding (Col 3:24–25).

If the above is true, Christians should be known, not just by our love (John 13:35), but also by our wisdom (Col 4:5). Interestingly, when the Jews in the Old Testament were in *foreign* lands, part of what made them stand out was their wisdom—for example, Joseph (Gen 41:39; Acts 7:10), Moses (Acts 7:22), Daniel (Dan 5:11), and Ezra (Ezra 7:25). Similarly, in the New Testament Jesus promised wisdom to his disciples so that they could stand up for him (Luke 21:15). In the same way, now that we in the West are living in a culture that is increasingly post-Christian, we can be known for our wisdom. If our views on ethics have become, fairly or unfairly, a barrier to belief in the Christian worldview, perhaps it's time for our wisdom to become an entry to belief in the Christian worldview.

We can do this by accessing God's general revelation, which is available to all. Here we can gain much wisdom from the world of nonbelievers. Interestingly this is exactly what the Old Testament heroes did: Moses learned much wisdom from the Egyptians (Acts 7:22), and Daniel from the Babylonians (Dan 1:5). In the same way, we can make a special effort to attend seminars, listen to podcasts, and sign up for courses that are run by nonbelievers. Not only will this help us find easy common ground with our non-believing friends, because we're reading and listening to their authors and experts. But it will also open us up to a wider range of God's wisdom. For example, I've learned much by going to parenting courses run by experts, most of whom are not believers. I read the *New York Times* regularly. And I have a steady diet of podcasts, such as *Freakonomics, Invisibilia, Malcolm Gladwell, The Moth, Planet Money, Pop Culture Happy Hour, Radio Atlantic, Reply All, TED Talks,* and *This American Life.* And at the same time, we can access God's special revelation, not only through the Scriptures, but also through the blessings of being a believer, not least the Holy Spirit who lives inside us to change us and guide us.

If we put all of this together, we will have a way of life that is obviously wise to all. We will stand out—just like Joseph and Daniel stood out in their foreign lands. The evidence will be that our way of life simply works better. In the same way that my friends at the BBQ wanted to talk to me about lawns, we will find that our non-believing friends will *want* to talk to us about other weighty matters of wisdom. They will come to us and ask us for our views. For example, just the other day at work a nurse asked me, "How do you get your children to obey you?" And I was able to share with her some general wisdom on parenting. As another example, because I have been able to maintain a relatively healthy lifestyle of eating sensibly, daily exercise, cycling, and surfing, many of my friends ask me for advice on eating and exercise. Moreover, we will find a ready audience that wants to listen to weighty matters of wisdom. In my work with City Bible Forum, I often give talks to downtown city workers on midlife crises, parenting, work-life balance, burnout, leadership, grieving, and finding purpose in work.

Hopefully you can see how wisdom provides an entry point into conversations about weighty matters. But it's more than that. Our wise way of life also makes what we say to be more plausible. I believe that when we in the West were part of a Christianized culture, we used to argue and teach in this sequence: (1) what I say is *true*; (2) if it's true, then you must *believe* it; and (3) if you believe it, you must *live* it. While this is the correct ontological sequence, now that we're part of post-Christian cultures, a better pedagogical sequence to help our friends discover this might be: (1) what you see is a wiser way to *live*; (2) but if it's a wiser way to live, then it's also more *believable*; (3) but if it's believable; you need to consider that it might also be *true*.

I love how in recent times, this expression has become popular: "How's that working for you?" If you're not familiar with this expression, it's actually a derogative put-down. Let's say your friend says, "I've decided not to sleep so I can spend more time watching late-night television," or "I've been on a popcorn-only diet for the last month," or "I'm not going to study for the exam." This is where you say, "So how's that working for you?" The implied message is that your friend is doing something unwise so it can't possibly be working well for them.

Conversely, if we live wisely, by and large it *should* work well for us. When this happens, just like with the lawn expert, people will want to listen to us. They will bring up weighty matters and want to hear what we have to say. By being wise, we create opportunities for these conversations. And we will make the Christian worldview more plausible.

9

BECOME THE DE FACTO CHAPLAIN IN THEIR LIVES

MY FRIEND CRAIG is a military chaplain. He spent a few years with his unit of soldiers when they were deployed in Afghanistan. There, his unit experienced many of the tragedies of war. As a result, he was often called upon to conduct funerals, provide counseling, and comfort the soldiers. But the commanding officer of this unit was an atheist—a strict, outspoken, nonbeliever. He had no time for religion or other such nonsense. But one day the commanding officer asked Craig to come into his office and to close the door behind him. The unit had gone through a few troubling weeks of trauma and tragedy that left them raw with hurt. The commanding officer asked Craig to sit down. Then he looked Craig in the eyes for a long time before finally saying, "I need you to pray for me." And so Craig did.

My chaplain friends—military, hospital, or school—say this is very normal. They tell me that our secular friends can be very firm in their non-belief. But there will be times of crisis that cry out for a transcendent act or word, in order for anything to make sense. And it's at those moments where they turn to you, the chaplain, to be that transcendent voice. They want (and need!) you to speak on behalf of God. To give some meaning and coherency. To perform a sacred ritual.

In our present secular age, Christians have the opportunity to be the unofficial de facto chaplains to our skeptical friends. This is exactly what happened to my friend Peter. He and his wife have invested time, over the last few years, to get to know a family from work. They've gone to their parties, and they've invited them over to their place for meals. Recently, the family lost a loved one, and they rang up Peter, basically to be comforted. They also asked Peter to say some words at the funeral. And they asked Peter to speak to their grandson, over the phone (with all the other members of the family listening in!) about whether or not his grandmother was in heaven or hell. A few weeks after the funeral, Peter and his wife visited the family at their home and provided a meal. When Peter told me this story, I said to him, "Can you see what's happened? You became their unofficial, de facto chaplain!"

At my work as a doctor in the hospital, I similarly take an interest in my work friends' lives. I ask them about what they've got planned for the weekend. But I go further than this. The following week, I'll resume the conversation and ask them about what they told me they were going to do for the weekend. They are astonished that I remembered! I also ask them about their family. But I go further than this. I'll remember the names of their children, what sports they play, and what grade they're in at school. So I can resume the conversation and ask, "So how did Dan do in his school basketball game?" And they're astonished that I remembered. I will also make sure I greet all the cleaners by name and treat them as equally important members of the health care team. Can you see what's happening? Bit by bit, I'm showing that I care about their personal lives, in a pastoral and appropriate way.

After I've earned enough trust, I can start asking things like, "How's Dan doing at school?" And I can follow up with questions that invite them to be more open, like, "How are things at home?" And then, if they feel like talking, I can ask more probing questions, "How does that make you feel?" or "How are you coping with it?" Bit by bit, I'm showing that I'm a caring and empathetic ear. And bit by bit they will start opening up to me about the concerns of life. Because, bit by bit, I have positioned myself into their lives as their unofficial, de facto chaplain.

10

LOOK FOR "BLACK SWAN" MOMENTS

IN 2007, NASSIM Nicholas Taleb wrote *The Black Swan: The Impact of the Highly Improbable.* This groundbreaking book spent almost a year in the *New York Times* bestseller list. In this book, Taleb argues that many momentous events are outliers that could not have been predicted. These events occur tangentially, and were not even what the discoverers were looking for in the first place. For example, no one discovered penicillin by planning to look for this antibiotic. Instead, it was "discovered" as a random accident, when Dr. Alexander Fleming found that the mold on his petri dish unexpectantly killed bacteria. Taleb's book concludes that we should embrace the seemingly randomness of life's events and just go out there and see what happens. We won't find what we're looking for, but something else that we're not looking for will find us.

Much of evangelism occurs the same way. Often we go out looking for opportunities to evangelize, but they just don't happen. Instead, we should just go out there—*and be Jesus to the community*—and the opportunities to evangelize will find us.

For example, a few years ago my wife Stephanie was in a busy shopping mall, along with our three young boys—at that stage aged three, five, and seven. It was crowded and late in the afternoon (after school). The boys were tired and hungry. But Steph noticed that there was a young Asian lady, holding her baby daughter, who was extremely distressed. So Steph asked this lady, who is called Holly, if everything was OK. Holly replied that she could not find her elderly mother, who could not speak any English, in the crowded shopping mall. Worse, the mother had the baby stroller—along with Holly's purse, money, mobile phone, and food for the baby!

Steph offered to help Holly look for her mother. So they spent the next 2–3 hours looking for the mother. This included walking up and down the shopping mall, visiting other shops outside of the mall, and even calling the police to report her missing. During this time, Steph offered food to Holly so she could feed her hungry baby. Finally, after almost giving up, they found the mother. Holly, of course, thanked Steph profusely for her time. But at that moment, Steph was also able to invite Holly to come to the playgroup at our church.

So Holly started coming to our church's playgroup. From there we invited Holly to come to our church. Holly's husband, Chris, was also so thankful to Steph that he accompanied Holly to our church. When Chris saw all the happy families worshiping at the church, he said to Holly, "Whatever these people believe, we also have to believe the same thing!"

We also invited Holly to come to our small group for adults, which meets at our home for lunch after Sunday church service. So Holly came to our home. That day we had a large BBQ for all the families at our church. Holly was intrigued. Being a new immigrant to Australia, she also wanted to learn how to host a BBQ at her own place. So we offered to help her and supplied her with our BBQ.

So Holly hosted a BBQ at her place. She invited families from our church's playgroup and families from a different (non-church) playgroup that she also attended. Here, most of the families were nonbelievers. As a result, many nonbelievers were able to meet believers at the BBQ, chat, and form new friendships. The flow-on effects from Holly's BBQ have been astounding. For example, one couple that we met at the BBQ has become our friends. Not only that, they are now starting to attend a local church with another Christian couple that they met at Holly's BBQ.

As another example, shortly after Holly's BBQ one of the couples suffered a tragedy—the husband was injured in a motorbike accident and became a quadriplegic. As a result of that accident, the couple was able to meet our church's pastor and his wife who suffered a similar tragedy—our pastor was also in a motorcycle accident and is now himself a quadriplegic. And as another result of the accident, the couple have started coming to my wife's midweek Bible study group with other mothers.

Can you see what has happened? At least three couples are now checking out Jesus, all because my wife Steph stopped to help Holly at a shopping mall a few years ago. This is not what Steph had in mind at the time. Back then she was only going out of her way to help a distressed shopper. She was being Jesus to the other woman. But that one act triggered a set of unforeseen, tangential, sequences of events that resulted in evangelism. This is exactly what Taleb would call a "Black Swan" moment.

Maybe we can do the same thing. In addition to our efforts to *do evangelism*—i.e., create opportunities for evangelism—we need also to *be Jesus*, and evangelism opportunities might come and find us tangentially in unforeseen and exciting ways.

CONCLUSION

I N MUCH OF the Bible, we see God's people working out how to be foreigners in a foreign land. In the Old Testament, we have at least Joseph, Moses, Daniel, Esther, Ezra, Nehemiah, and Jonah. And in the New Testament, we have Peter in Caesarea and Paul in his missionary journeys—particularly before foreign powers (e.g., Agrippa) and audiences (e.g., the Areopagus in Athens). It seems that a key part of our identity as God's people is knowing how to be foreigners (see 1 Pet 1:1).

Interestingly, part of being a foreigner is also knowing how to speak up when it matters. On the one hand, this is never an easy thing to do. For example, Moses worried that he wasn't gifted enough to speak (Exod 4:10). Nehemiah was very much afraid of the King's anger (Neh 2:1–3). Esther similarly feared for her life (Esth 4:11). On the other hand, often this is exactly why God has placed us in these situations, so that we can speak up. Mordecai's words to Esther might also be for us: "Who knows but that you have come to your royal position for such a time as this?" (Esth 4:14).

Perhaps "For Such a Time as This" can be our motto. We live in interesting times. Our friends are more skeptical than ever. In much of the Western world, we are now post-Christian, post-churched, post-reached, post-millennial, and post-anything-else-that-we-can-think-of! But these are also exciting times. Jesus promised his followers that one day we would have to speak up for him (see Luke 21:12–13). What we might think of as threats to our witness are actually God-given opportunities to speak on his behalf. Hopefully the above ten tips might free you up and empower you in your identity and activity as a witness for Christ.

Acknowledgments

T HE SERIES Questions for Restless Minds is produced by the Christ on Campus Initiative, under the stewardship of the editorial board of D. A. Carson (senior editor), Douglas Sweeney, Graham Cole, Dana Harris, Thomas McCall, Geoffrey Fulkerson, and Scott Manetsch. The editorial board recognizes with gratitude the many outstanding evangelical authors who have contributed to this series, as well as the sponsorship of Trinity Evangelical Divinity School (Deerfield, Illinois), and the financial support of the MAC Foundation and the Carl F. H. Henry Center for Theological Understanding. The editors also wish to thank Christopher Gow, who created the study questions accompanying each book, and Todd Hains, our editor at Lexham Press. May God alone receive the glory for this endeavor!

Study Guide Questions

1. What are some practical ways that you can practice hospitality this week?

2. Work on this together: what are some questions you could use to take conversation from the layer of interests to values? From values to worldview?

3. Chan refers frequently to storytelling as a disarming way of sharing about Jesus. What stories do you have from your own life that would be good ways to share about Jesus? What gospel stories could you tell that communicate who Jesus was and what he accomplished?

4. How does Chan address common Western worldview assumptions? Are there any critiques or questions that you find particularly insightful?

5. What does Chan mean by positive apologetics?

6. Is there anyone in your life for whom you are a de facto chaplain? How can you love these people well and build trust?

7. Take turns and spend two minutes sharing about your commitment to Jesus to one another. As the listener, practice hearing, understanding, and feeling what your partner is saying, and ask one or two follow-up questions.

For Further Reading

Dillon, Christine. *Telling the Gospel Through Story: Evangelism That Keeps Hearers Wanting More.* IVP, 2012.

> My friend John G, a returning missionary from Asia, was once asked by his seminary, "What's one thing you wish you'd learned from seminary that would have really helped your ministry?" John immediately replied, "How to tell the Gospel as story." This is because 90 percent of the majority world are oral learners rather than literate ones. They prefer to learn from a story than from a book or lecture. But the astonishing thing is that 80 percent of the Western world is the same! For many of us, our preferred learning style is also from story. That means that one of the best ways to talk to our friends is through story. And one of the best resources for this is Dillon's *Telling the Gospel Through Story* and the accompanying website www.storyingthe scriptures.com.

Keller, Timothy. *Making Sense of God: Finding God in the Modern World.* Viking, 2016.

> In the last ten years, many of our non-believing friends no longer even know what it is that Christians believe. Their problems with the Christian faith isn't that they have "defeater beliefs" (e.g., how can a loving God allow suffering?). Nor is their problem that they don't know what to believe. They don't even know *why* they would need to believe something as outrageous as the Christian God. Keller's *Making Sense of God* helps our friends to see that much of what we believe as *a priori* truths—such as human rights, equality, justice, identity, purpose—can only be true if the Christian God exists. Thus, for both believers and non-believers alike, we *need* the Christian God to be true.

Keller, Timothy. *Reason for God: Belief in an Age of Skepticism.* Penguin Books, 2008.

> Some of our non-believing friends, who are familiar with the Christian faith, will have "defeater beliefs" that stop them from believing in the Christian truth claims. For example, they might be asking, "How can a loving God send people to hell?" Or "Aren't all religions the same?" In the first half of *Reason for God*, Keller engages with these defeater beliefs and gently addresses them. In the second half of this book, Keller provides reasons for why the Christian

claims (the resurrection, the reliability of the Bible, the person of Jesus, etc.) are trustworthy and should be believed.

Murray, Abdu. *Saving Truth: Finding Meaning and Clarity in a Post-Truth World.* Zondervan, 2018.

Christian and non-Christian views in the West seem further apart than ever before. So how can we bridge such separate worldviews? Murray's *Saving Truth* helps us navigate this new post-Christian world. He explains how we've come to a post-truth society. He then shows how the Christian world-view is essential for the very things that our friends hold to be true—i.e., human dignity and freedom.

Newman, Randy. *Questioning Evangelism: Engaging People's Hearts the Way Jesus Did.* Kregal, 2004.

The art of conversation is not to talk, but to ask questions and listen. In a good conversation we actually do very little talking. That means, when we talk to our friends about things that matter, it's rare that we get a chance to talk without interruptions. Instead, in order to talk to our friends, we need to learn the art of asking questions. Newman's *Questioning Evangelism* gives some guidelines on how to ask questions that will help our friends see the presuppositions behind their beliefs and expose the true question behind their questions.

Chan, Sam. *Evangelism in a Skeptical World: How to Make the Unbelievable News about Jesus More Believable.* Zondervan, 2018.

> The methods for evangelism that once worked decades ago no longer seem as effective in the twenty-first century. My book, *Evangelism in a Skeptical World*, offers fresh suggestions for evangelism. It applies insights from missiology—cultural analysis, contextualization, storytelling—to evangelism. These methods have been field-tested in universities, high schools, conferences, and cafés. And they work. They get past the hearer's sceptical posture so that they can seriously consider the good news of Jesus.

Spufford, Francis. *Unapologetic: Why, Despite Everything, Christianity Can Still Make Surprising Emotional Sense.* HarperCollins, 2012.

> Unlike me, who is a Christian trying to become a writer, Spufford is the opposite! He is a writer who became a Christian. Spufford was once an atheist, but he recently converted to the Christian faith. He writes *Unapologetic* to explain to his non-believing friends why he made this transition into faith. This is a helpful book because it gives insights into how someone might decide to become a Christian. It also gives insights into how someone might explain this to their skeptical friends.

Notes

1. I owe much of the observations in this point to Andrew Katay, who is a pastor in Sydney, Australia.
2. I learned this particular question from Wendy Potts and Stephen Dinning, who are evangelists in the Wollongong area of Sydney.
3. I learned this question from my friend L-T Hopper. I heard him casually ask this question to our server at a café. Interestingly, our server wasn't offended at all by the question. Instead, he sheepishly answered, "No, but I know I should." These days, people might not yet want to know about the Christian faith, but they also know they should be pursuing some spiritual connection.

LEXHAM PRESS